292
GER

Gerstein, Mordicai

Tales of Pan

DATE DUE

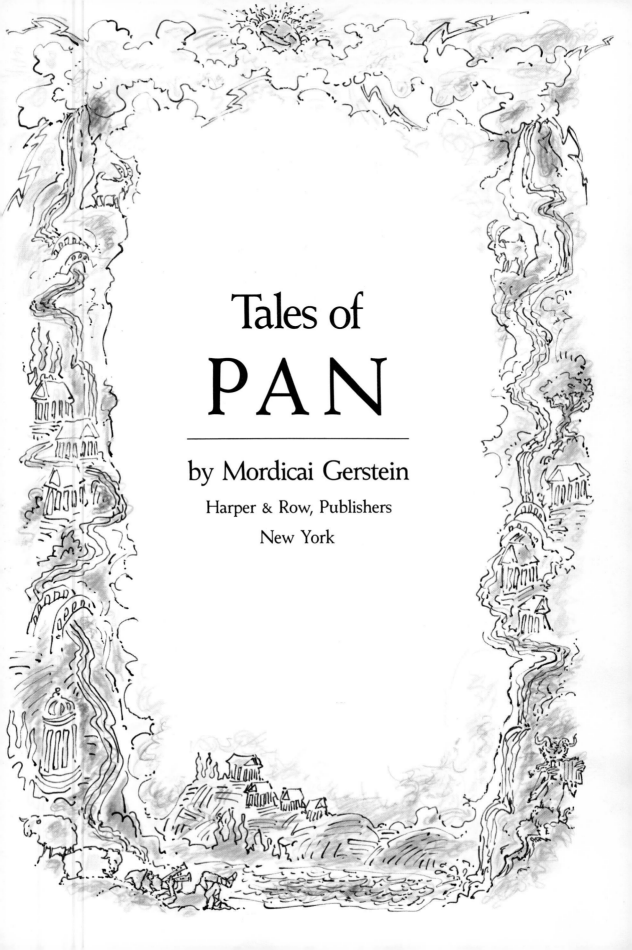

Tales of
PAN

by Mordicai Gerstein

Harper & Row, Publishers

New York

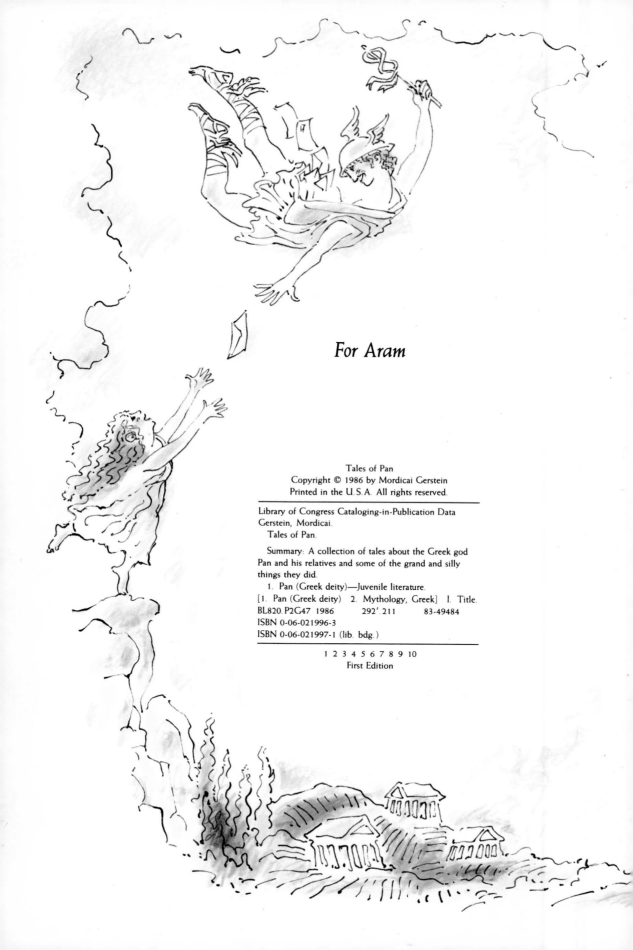

For Aram

Tales of Pan
Copyright © 1986 by Mordicai Gerstein
Printed in the U.S.A. All rights reserved.

Library of Congress Cataloging-in-Publication Data
Gerstein, Mordicai.
  Tales of Pan.

  Summary: A collection of tales about the Greek god
Pan and his relatives and some of the grand and silly
things they did.
  1. Pan (Greek deity)—Juvenile literature.
[1. Pan (Greek deity) 2. Mythology, Greek] I. Title.
BL820.P2G47 1986   292′.211   83-49484
ISBN 0-06-021996-3
ISBN 0-06-021997-1 (lib. bdg.)

1 2 3 4 5 6 7 8 9 10
First Edition

CONTENTS

FOREWORD

Long, long ago, a family of gods lived in ancient Greece. They lived on top of Mount Olympus, under great craggy clouds that looked like whipped cream.

Zeus, the thunder god, was the king and father of most of them. His many children had children, and they all had uncles and aunts and lots of cousins. They were all gods of one thing or another. Most of the books about them tell us how great, grand, and powerful they were. But they could also be stupid, bad tempered, and silly, just like any other family.

The god Pan was one of them. He wasn't the greatest or grandest god. He didn't want to be. He certainly wasn't the best looking. But he was the silliest, and the one that delighted the hearts of all the others.

The ancient Greeks sang hymns to Pan.

"All hail to Pan," they sang. "Goat-footed, two-horned lover of noisy confusion!" They made him offerings of wine and honey, but they also liked to joke and tell stories about him and his relatives behind their backs.

Here are some of those stories about Pan and his family and the grand and silly things they did.

THE BIRTH OF PAN

It was not on Mount Olympus but in a beautiful gardenlike valley in Arcadia that Pan was born. While his father Hermes, the quick messenger of the gods, was rushing around the world delivering the mail, Pan was getting ready to make his appearance. The midwife listened at his mother Dryope's belly for the baby's heart.

"I don't believe it!" she yelped, falling off her chair. "I hear giggles and snickering!"

Pan was born a minute later. He came out laughing, shouting, and kicking his little legs in all directions. When the nurse saw that they were goat legs, she screamed. She ran out the door smack into Hermes, who was just getting home.

"Is it a boy or a girl?" Hermes asked her.

The nurse screamed again. Then she ran down the road and out of sight. Hermes rushed in and his happy wife showed him their new son.

His heart filled with joy when he saw that along with the goat legs, the baby had two curly little horns growing out of his forehead, and a curly little beard on his chin.

"This is the son I've always wanted!" cried Hermes, kissing his wife. He took the baby in his arms, all wrapped in mountain rabbit skins, and flew right through the roof.

Hermes flew straight to Mount Olympus to show off his son to the other gods. He put the baby right in Zeus's lap.

"What is this?" asked Zeus, unwrapping the rabbit skins.

The baby jumped up laughing and kicked Zeus in the nose. Zeus looked at him and began to laugh too. Then all the gods began to laugh. They passed the baby around and even Hera, the crabby queen, had to smile. They called him Pan because he delighted all their hearts. Pan means all.

PAN LEAVES OLYMPUS

There were quarrels and occasional screaming fights, but usually Olympus was a fairly peaceful place. Pan arrived and changed it.

He climbed up and down the pillars and galloped through the throne rooms shrieking. He threw Zeus's thunderbolts at Queen Hera. He used Uncle Apollo's harp to shoot Aunt Artemis's arrows at Uncle Ares. He laughed and made confetti out of Hermes's mail. At one day old, he was the fully grown god of noise and confusion.

"He delights my heart, but he'll drive me mad!" complained Zeus to Hermes.

"He's a menace!" shrilled Queen Hera. "And the palace looks and smells like a goat pen!"

All Pan heard from his family was "Shush!" or "Be serious!" or "Grow up!"

He tried to do as they asked. He practiced sitting on his throne but it was boring. He wandered through the palace with its endless towering pillars and he felt lonely. Then he looked down at Arcadia where he'd been born. It was green and sparkling in the summer sun.

"That's where I belong!" said Pan. And with one great leap, and a howl that rocked the palace, Pan left Olympus.

All the other gods sighed a great sigh of relief. Pan landed in Arcadia, *splash!* right in the middle of a giggling stream.

"This is more like it," he said.

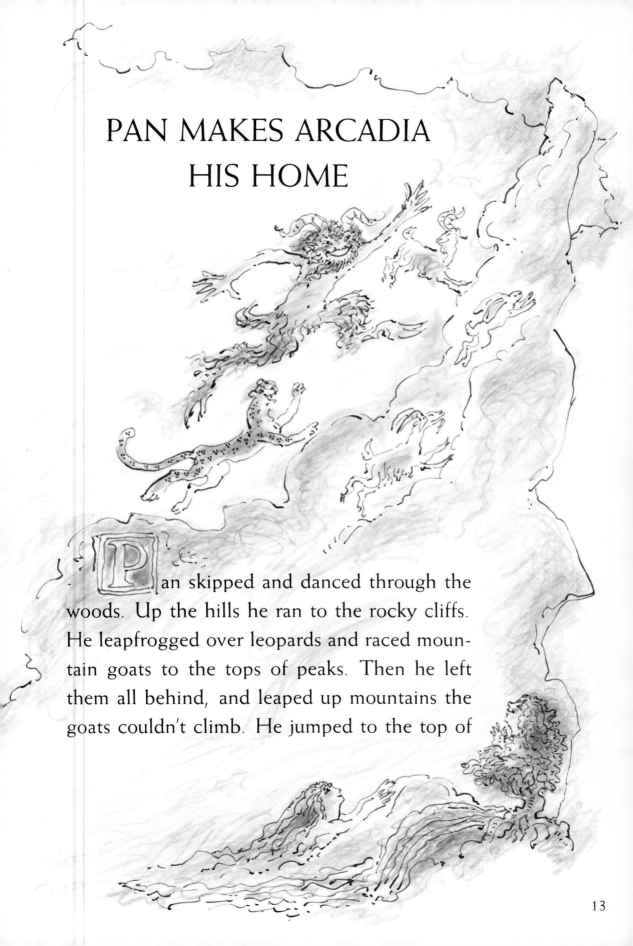

PAN MAKES ARCADIA
HIS HOME

Pan skipped and danced through the woods. Up the hills he ran to the rocky cliffs. He leapfrogged over leopards and raced mountain goats to the tops of peaks. Then he left them all behind, and leaped up mountains the goats couldn't climb. He jumped to the top of

the highest, rockiest, snowcapped peak, and there Pan caught his breath and looked around. He could see all of Arcadia. There were nymphs everywhere: beautiful spirits of tree, flower, and fountain. He saw wild animals and birds of all kinds. Far below he saw hunters, shepherds, and beekeepers.

And because each god had to look after something, Pan decided to look after all of them. *"Yahooo!"* he yowled, and jumped for joy.

Then he skipped down the mountain, clapping and whistling to all the people and creatures of Arcadia.

"I am Pan!" he shouted. "I am a new god! From now on shepherds will never lose their sheep, nor sheep their shepherds. All the hives will overflow with honey, and hunters will never go hungry!"

All the people, creatures, and nymphs, danced after him, clapping and cheering.

He showed them how to build proper shrines to him, and how to leave him offerings of honey, roast venison, red wine, and flowers. He watched delighted as they went off and did as he'd told them. Pan stretched and scratched his back against a tree. Then he smiled, curled up in the cool grass and took a nap.

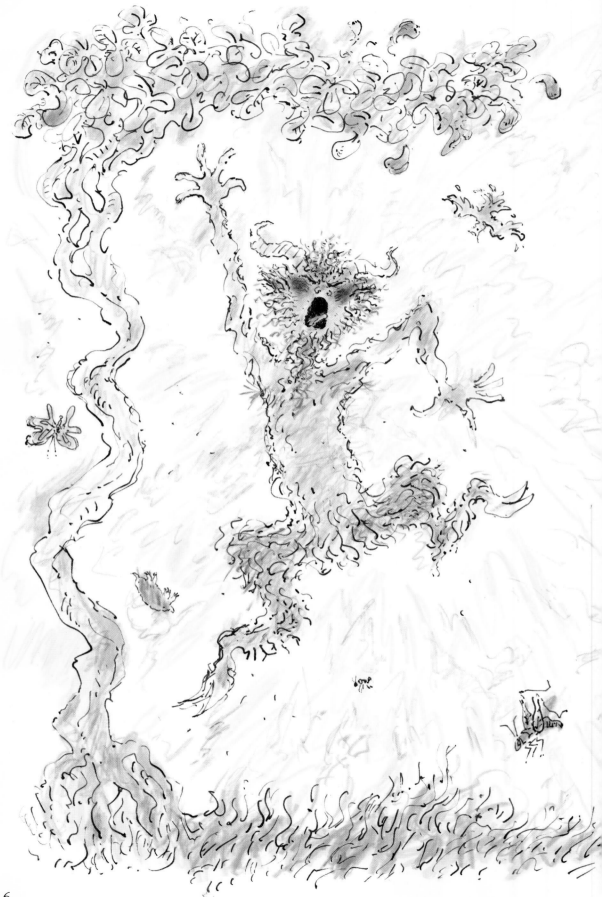

PAN SHOUTS AND INVENTS PANIC

an loved noise and confusion, but he also loved his afternoon naps. When Pan napped, all Arcadia, birds, beasts, and beekeepers, had to walk on tiptoe and whisper.

One afternoon while Pan was napping under a fig tree, an ant with a cold tiptoed by. When the ant sneezed, Pan jumped up and shouted: "CAN'TYOUSEEI'MSLEEPINGKEEPTHENOISEDOWN!"

It was the loudest, most surprising shout ever heard. All the sheep in Arcadia jumped straight up, their wool stuck straight out, and they ran off in every direction, while the shepherds ran in circles, and all the birds, butterflies, and bees zoomed from one end of Arcadia to the other, bumping into the rabbits, foxes, and nymphs, who got all tangled in the trees, bushes, and vines. Even Echo, way up in her craggy canyon, was so startled she was speechless.

It was a day and a half before everyone calmed down, and the ant that started it all was

never seen again. Pan himself was very impressed.

"What was that?" the people and creatures all asked each other.

"I call it *panic!*" said Pan, proudly. "I just invented it!"

From then on Pan used this special shout whenever someone disturbed his naps. Sometimes he used it against enemies, or to help friends or relatives in trouble. Other times he used it to scare people out of their wits, just for fun. At one time or another, everyone got a taste of "panic."

PAN FALLS IN LOVE
WITH THE MOON

After a while Pan grew lonely up on his craggy mountain peaks. One night he looked up and fell in love with the moon.

"Oh, beautiful moon," he called up to her, "please marry me!"

The moon was very proud.

"You're too ugly!" she said to him.

He howled to her, he cried to her, but it was no use. She wouldn't even shine on him. Pan's heart was breaking, but he wouldn't give

up. One cloudless night, he dressed himself up
like a woolly lamb, in a special fleece he had
made. It looked so soft and was so white and
beautiful, the moon was dazzled.

"Where are you going, little lamb?" she
asked, pouring moonbeams onto his back.

"*Baa baa baa,*" said Pan, leading the moon
into the woods. She followed, scattering moonbeams in the darkest places.

"Oh, moon, I'm just a little lamb. Will you
marry me?" baa'd Pan.

When she recognized his voice, the moon
was furious. She ran and hid behind the earth's
shadow, and it was weeks before she came out
to shine again. It was the first eclipse.

Pan cried and tore his hair.

"I'll never fall in love again!" he wailed.

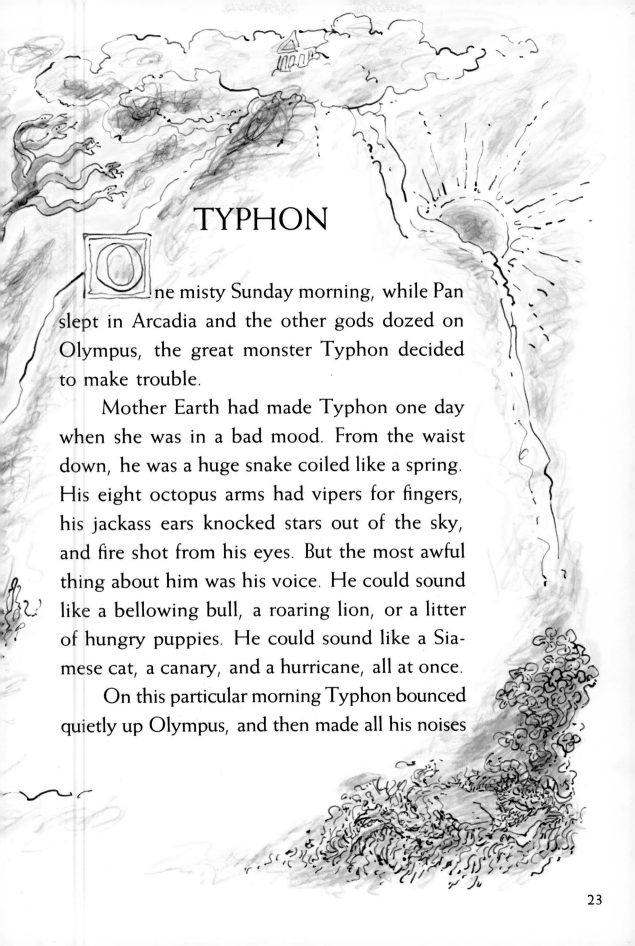

TYPHON

One misty Sunday morning, while Pan slept in Arcadia and the other gods dozed on Olympus, the great monster Typhon decided to make trouble.

Mother Earth had made Typhon one day when she was in a bad mood. From the waist down, he was a huge snake coiled like a spring. His eight octopus arms had vipers for fingers, his jackass ears knocked stars out of the sky, and fire shot from his eyes. But the most awful thing about him was his voice. He could sound like a bellowing bull, a roaring lion, or a litter of hungry puppies. He could sound like a Siamese cat, a canary, and a hurricane, all at once.

On this particular morning Typhon bounced quietly up Olympus, and then made all his noises at once. Zeus and his family were so frightened they ran all the way to Egypt and disguised themselves as animals. Zeus took the shape of a ram, Apollo a crow, Hera a cow, and Hermes an ibis. Some people think this is why the Egyptians worshipped these animals for years after. Only Athena, Zeus's gray-eyed daughter, wasn't afraid.

"You should be ashamed of yourself!" she said to her father.

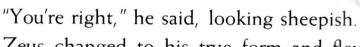

"You're right," he said, looking sheepish.

Zeus changed to his true form and flew back to Olympus in a storm. Typhon was devouring the palace when Zeus hit him with a thunderbolt. Typhon howled and then made

the sound of a flock of ducks flying south. Zeus was so startled, he couldn't move for a moment. In that moment, Typhon grabbed the sinews that held Zeus's muscles together, and Zeus collapsed like a suit with no one wearing it.

Typhon took the sinews to his cave. He put a rug on top of them and lay down on the rug for a nap. Now the family was really worried.

"What do we do now?" they asked one another.

Then Hermes remembered his son Pan. Pan was showering in a fountain when Hermes flew down and told him what had happened.

"*Yaahooo!*" whooped Pan.

He hopped on Hermes's shoulders and they flew to Typhon's cave. Typhon was snoring, making a sound like a herd of pigs and a hive of bees. Pan tiptoed right up to his ear, took a deep breath, and let out his loudest, most horrible shout:

"BBLLLRRRRRRRGGGGGRRROOOOOOOOAAAAA
AAAAWWWWWWWWWWLLLLLLRRGAH!"

It sounded like the beginning and end of the world. Typhon shot up into the air. Quickly Hermes reached under the rug and grabbed Zeus's sinews. Pan and Hermes flew back to Zeus and helped him put them on before Typhon hit the ground.

"Now I'm angry!" growled Zeus, flexing his muscles. "Pan, hitch the winged horses to my chariot, and hand me those thunderbolts."

With Pan riding piggyback and shouting, Zeus chased Typhon roaring across Greece and part of Italy. Zeus threw thunderbolts, and Typhon threw mountains back at them as he ran. When they got to Sicily, Zeus picked up Mount Aetna and dropped it on Typhon's head. That was the end of the battle.

Pan, Zeus, and Hermes flew home for dinner, and everyone cheered. To this day, fire and smoke come out of Mount Aetna, not to mention some very strange noises.

PAN FALLS IN LOVE
WITH QUEEN OMPHALE
AND MEETS HERCULES

From a high
rocky cliff, Pan looked down and
saw the beautiful Queen Omphale
walking in her garden.

"From now on, I love only Queen
Omphale!" he crowed, turning somersaults.

"But, Pan," the brook nymphs giggled as
he danced past, "Queen Omphale is in love with
the hero Hercules, and he's in love with her."

"One kiss from me," cried Pan, skipping down the mountain, "and she'll forget that pea-brained oaf exists!"

The hero Hercules was part human and part god. He was seven feet tall, and wore the skin of a lion he'd killed with one kick. Even as an infant in his crib, he'd strangled two fire-breathing snakes, one in each hand.

Queen Omphale and Hercules were getting ready for a costume ball at her palace. For costumes they decided to wear each other's clothes. Queen Omphale put on Hercules's lion

skin, and he put on her gold and purple gown
with the puffed sleeves and little silver girdle.
When they looked in the big mirror they burst
into laughter. Every time they looked at each
other, they'd start laughing again. Finally, Omphale went to have her hair done, and Hercules,
still giggling, lay down on her couch for a nap.
Just as the sun was setting, Hercules started to
snore, and Pan hopped through the window.

Pan had come to ask Omphale to marry
him, and to carry her back to the mountains.
The room was filling with shadows, but Pan saw

the figure in purple and gold on Omphale's couch. He also heard the snoring.

"My love is sleeping," he whispered to himself. "I'll wake her with a kiss."

He tiptoed over and gave Hercules a big kiss that woke him instantly. Hercules looked at Pan and Pan looked at Hercules. With a great roar, Hercules picked Pan up by his tail, swung him three times around the room, and threw him out the window.

"Look!" said one sparrow to another. "The great god Pan has learned to fly!"

Pan landed in a heap on the same craggy cliff he'd left earlier. There he sat with his head in his hands and an aching heart.

HOW PAN MADE HIS PIPES AND MARRIED ECHO

In the spring, Pan fell in love with nymphs. There were water nymphs, tree nymphs, flower, fountain, and mountain nymphs, and many more. They were all lovely.

First Pan fell in love with one, then he fell in love with two or three. He chased them through woods and pastures, and they ran giggling and screaming. Then they chased him over fields and mountains, and he ran shouting and laughing. It was great fun.

One May morning, Pan was chasing a fig tree nymph named Syrinx.

"From now on, I love only you!" he yelled.

"You smell like a goat!" she yelled back.

He chased her all over Arcadia. Finally Syrinx found herself on a riverbank with Pan close behind her. She was tired of running and she didn't want to have anything to do with him. She called to the river nymphs, "Sisters! Help me!"

Pan ran up and threw his arms around her, but he found himself with an armful of reeds. The river nymphs had changed Syrinx into a river reed.

Poor Pan cried and sighed, and his sighing whistled through the reeds and made a beautiful mournful sound. He didn't know which reed was Syrinx, so he took several of different lengths, tied them together, and made them into pipes. Then he sat down by the river and played music on them.

"I'll call them Syrinx," he said.

All Arcadia was quiet and listened.

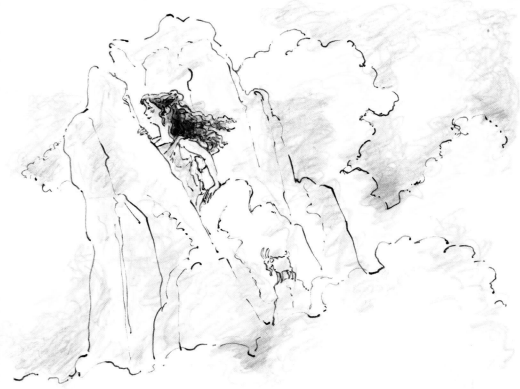

The music of Pan's pipes was so sweet, and
so sad and beautiful, that he charmed shy Echo.
She came down from her lonely perch above
the clouds and sang along with him.

They were soon married and had a lovely
little daughter named Iynx.

IYNX PLAYS PRANKS

Iynx was lovely like her mother Echo, and high-spirited like her father Pan, but mostly, she took after her grandfather Hermes. She loved to eavesdrop and play pranks.

For fun one day, she cast a spell on Great-Grandpa Zeus. She made him fall in love with Io, the daughter of a river god. She looked a bit like a hippopotamus and was a good friend of Queen Hera. Zeus found himself in the middle of a river telling Io he was mad about her.

"I'm shocked!" gasped Io, turning red. "Wait till I tell Hera about this!"

Meanwhile Iynx told Queen Hera where Zeus was, and hid so she could watch the fun.

Zeus heard Hera coming.

"She musn't find me with you!" he said to Io, and hurriedly changed the surprised Io into a white cow. It was all he could think of on the spur of the moment.

"Who is this cow?" demanded Hera, as she stepped out of her coach of golden clouds.

"T-this c-cow . . ." stammered Zeus, "is a s-surprise cow I got for YOU, my dear!"

"You must be up to something," Hera said, looking at the cow suspiciously. She didn't recognize her friend.

She called to her servant Argus, the hundred-eyed monster.

"Take this cow and don't let her out of your sight," she told him, and flew off on her errands.

Argus, who had as many teeth as eyes, tied Io in a muddy field of weeds. Then he sat and watched her. Io looked toward Olympus with rage in her eyes.

"Zeus! You get me out of here!" she bellowed, but all that came out was:

"MOOOOOOOOO!"

Zeus heard her and felt terrible.

"I can't understand why I acted such a fool in the first place," he said to himself.

"Maybe someone put a spell on you!" a little voice snickered.

Zeus looked under his throne and there was Iynx.

"So it was you, you little brat!" he growled, as he caught her by the ear.

"You need a spell put on you," said Zeus. "So you can stick your nose into a tree instead of other people's business!"

And with that, he turned Iynx into a woodpecker. Screeching, she flew home to Pan and Echo.

"Look what Great-Grandpa Zeus did to me!" she shrieked.

Echo shrieked too, and Pan called his father Hermes for help.

"Oh, no!" said Hermes, when he saw his granddaughter pecking her lunch from an oak tree.

"Oh, yes!" said Pan. "You've got to do something!"

Hermes flew to Olympus to see Zeus.

"I was just about to call you," said Zeus. "I need your help to change a cow back into the daughter of a river god."

Hermes agreed to help get Io away from Argus, and Zeus agreed to change Iynx back into herself.

"But no more pranks or I'll make her a bird for good," Zeus warned.

Then Zeus apologized to Io and changed her back into herself. It was weeks before she could talk without mooing, and she never spoke to Zeus again. It was all very confusing, but finally they all were back in their original forms.

Iynx, however, just couldn't stop playing tricks. A week later she made Zeus fall in love with a giraffe. This time he changed her into a woodpecker permanently, as he'd promised. Pan and Echo were very sad at first, but they soon got used to her new form and loved her as much as ever.

THE GREAT MUSIC CONTEST

Pan played his pipes day and night. He composed a special song for each nymph and flower, and a tune for each fountain and stream. Echo echoed his piping all over Arcadia.

"Not even my uncle Apollo, with his golden harp, can make music like mine!" sang Pan, as he danced on a rocky beach and piped to the waves.

On Olympus, meanwhile, Apollo was trying to tune his harp. He heard Pan's piping. He heard it day and night, and finally he'd had enough. He grabbed his harp, jumped out of his throne, and landed right next to Pan.

"Your noise is getting on my nerves!" snapped Apollo. "I can't even tune my harp."

"Noise?" sputtered Pan. "Your pathetic plunking is the noise! I make music!"

"You call your tuneless twittering music?" sneered Apollo. "You don't know what music is."

"Please don't fight!" boomed a great voice above them. "It hurts my ears."

It was the mountain, kindly old Mount Timolus.

"I suggest there be a music contest," said Timolus. "Pan's pipes against Apollo's harp, and I'll be the judge. I love music and I'm completely fair."

"Good!" said Pan.

"Great!" said Apollo. "Let's begin!"

"Wait a second," said the mountain.

He combed the clouds from his eyes and he cleared the trees and shrubs from his ears.

"That's better," he said, turning to Pan. "You may begin!"

Pan began to play, and all over Arcadia the rabbits danced with the foxes, and the crickets and goats and sheep sang along. The nymphs all danced with the trees and flowers. The fish danced in the sea; even the clams danced. All

the birds, bees, and butterflies twirled in the sky, and, of course, the people, from babies in their cradles to old folks on crutches, danced and did cartwheels.

When Pan had finished, the nymphs and shepherds all clapped and cheered.

"Bravo! Bravo Pan!" they cried.

"Shhh!" hissed Mount Timolus. "It's Apollo's turn."

Apollo stood up. The laurel leaves around his head brushed the edges of space, and his cape trailed in the Ionian Sea. He lifted his pick, and at the first note, the stars came out and began to dance in constellations. At the second note, the moon rose beaming and waltzed with the sun. And at the third note, the hills and

mountains danced with the valleys and all the flowers bloomed. The rivers of the world sang in a chorus, the Atlantic ocean danced with the Mediterranean sea, and the waves leaped over the rainbows that appeared everywhere. Whales swam blissfully across the sky, and the whole world laughed and cried with happiness.

"That's it!" cried Timolus, out of breath from dancing.

His old eyes sparkled with tears.

"Apollo wins!"

All the forests, nymphs, animals, and even Pan's mother Dryope agreed. Pan himself cried like a baby and took Apollo's hand. Pan still played his pipes after that, but for a while, he played a little more quietly.

KING MIDAS'S EARS

Old King Midas lived in Arcadia. He was proof that you don't have to be smart to be a king. He was famous for having asked the gods to make everything he touched turn to gold. For a joke they agreed. When bread became lumps of gold in his mouth and wine became liquid gold on his lips, he begged to be normal again.

Now he loved the simple life, eating nuts and berries, and following Pan through the woods like a puppy.

"O great Pan, please play your pipes!" he begged. "Not even gold can buy music like yours!"

"Oh, come on now," said Pan. "Everyone knows that Apollo's music puts mine to shame."

"Not to me," said Midas. "To my ears your music is sweeter, sillier, sadder, better, and more beautiful than any in the world."

"Is that so?" a voice rang out, accompanied by the strumming of a harp.

It was Apollo. He came once a week to give Pan music lessons.

"To your ears Pan's music is better than mine?" asked Apollo.

He bent down nose to nose with Midas.

"W-well, yes. . . ." stammered Midas. "Of course, that's only my opinion."

"Well, it's my opinion," said Apollo, "that you have the ears of a jackass!"

Suddenly the air was full of laughter. Midas was surrounded by nymphs pointing at him and giggling hysterically. He reached up, and sure enough, he had long furry jackass ears. He turned bright red, stuffed the ears under his king's hat, and ran home.

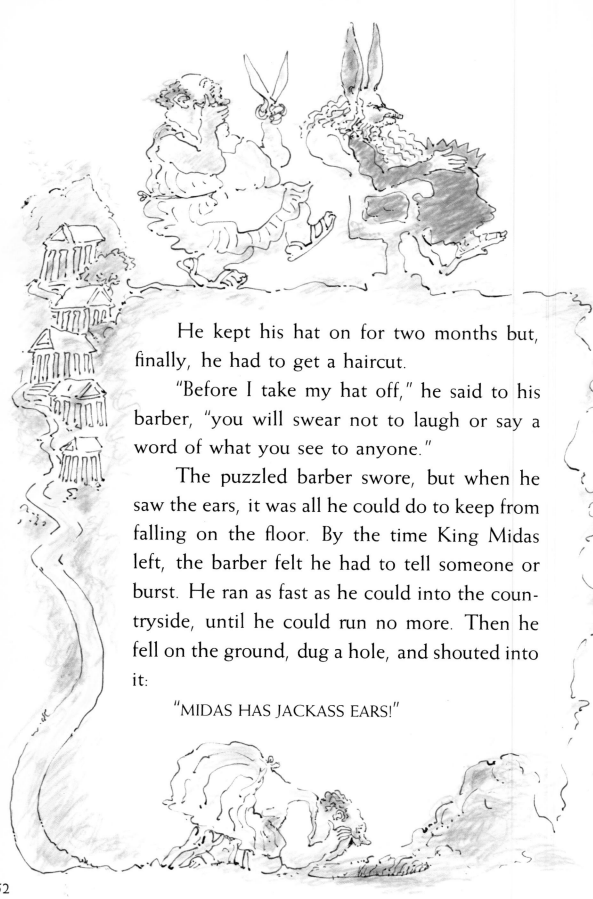

He kept his hat on for two months but, finally, he had to get a haircut.

"Before I take my hat off," he said to his barber, "you will swear not to laugh or say a word of what you see to anyone."

The puzzled barber swore, but when he saw the ears, it was all he could do to keep from falling on the floor. By the time King Midas left, the barber felt he had to tell someone or burst. He ran as fast as he could into the countryside, until he could run no more. Then he fell on the ground, dug a hole, and shouted into it:

"MIDAS HAS JACKASS EARS!"

He covered the hole and went home feeling relieved. But that night, his words sprouted in the ground, and by morning they'd grown into reeds. When the breeze blew, they rustled back and forth whispering.

"Midas has jackass ears. Midas has jackass ears," they whispered for all the world to hear.

Pan and Apollo heard up on Olympus, where they were practicing their music. They roared with laughter. Then they played a duet together.

PAN AT THE BATTLE OF MARATHON

As the years passed, the people heard Pan's pipes less and less. His daughter Iynx had flown off to make her own nest. Now Pan and Echo, happy to be alone together, stayed high above the clouds on the rocky peaks they loved. When they played music and sang, only the gods and mountain goats could hear them.

One day Pan looked down and was surprised to see that all over Greece his shrines were overgrown with weeds. Some had even fallen down.

"Echo, look! We've been forgotten!" he said.

"We've been forgotten," agreed Echo, as she always did.

Then Pan saw all the people gathering in Athens. They looked frightened, as if something were wrong. Pan called to his father Hermes. One could always get the news from him.

"The Greeks are at war with the Persians," said Hermes. "The Persians have a bigger, stronger army, and want to have a battle. Look there," Hermes pointed. "The Greeks have sent their fastest runner, Phidippides, to Sparta to ask for help."

Pan looked, and saw the runner Phidippides arrive in Sparta. He had run 150 miles in
24 hours without stopping, but the Spartan king
was not eager to help.

"I'm sorry, but we have problems of our
own," he said.

Phidippides had a drink of water and started
back to Athens with the bad news. He was
running at twilight through the high rocky hills
when he felt something running beside him,

something huge and shaggy with hooves and the smell of a goat. He turned his head but saw nothing. Then he heard a great chuckle echo around the rocky cliffs. When he looked again, Pan was running beside him.

"It makes me sad that your people have forgotten me," the god said as they ran. "I've always loved them. Build me a shrine in Athens, and I'll help you beat the Persians."

Phidippides blinked the sweat from his eyes, and Pan was gone. He ran all night, and as the sun rose, he entered Athens. He told the people what he had seen and heard.

They built a shrine to Pan that morning, and they piled it high with honey, roast venison, flowers, and red wine.

The battle started in the afternoon, in a field called Marathon. The sound of Persian swords beating back Greek shields was suddenly drowned out by a terrific shout.

"GGGRRRRAAAOOOWWLLLRRROOOAAARRR!"

It sounded like the beginning and end of the world. The Greeks knew what it was, but the Persians turned pale and their knees shook. Then they turned and ran in every direction, falling over each other in "panic."

The battle was over, and the Greeks cheered. Phidippides's long run was called the run of Marathon, after the field where the battle took place.

He and Pan were remembered and loved in Athens for many years after that. But Pan lost interest in people again. He preferred Echo and the snowcapped peaks. He lay on his back and piped for the eagles.

THE DEATH OF PAN

The centuries rolled by like a parade of clouds along the horizon. People sailed new seas, fought new wars, and built new cities. The world grew bigger and Greece looked smaller. There were new gods to worship. People rarely looked to Mount Olympus for help anymore.

Sometimes, when there was a thunderstorm, people would look up and say, "There's old Zeus. Whatever became of him and his family?"

One stormy night around the time of the birth of Jesus, a sailor named Thammus was on the deck of his ship. He heard wailing and crying in the wind. Then a voice in the thunder boomed, "Pan is dead! The great god Pan is dead!"

When Thammus got to shore he told people what he'd heard. Some people believed it
and wept. Some didn't. And some just shrugged.

"There was no Pan," the shruggers said.
"He was just a myth."

Some people think that Zeus and his family have become the planets that bear their Roman names. Hermes became Mercury, Zeus became Jupiter, and the others the rest of the planets. Others say that on clear nights, the gods act out their battles and pranks in the constellations. There are even those who believe Pan and Zeus and the rest are still living in Greece around Mount Olympus.

"They're in disguise," they say. "You can't tell them from any other family."

But what disguise could Pan wear? Even if he hid his hooves and covered his horns, how could he hide his grin on bee-buzzing, bird-singing spring mornings?

On mornings like that, when you feel like leaping and shouting, YAAAAHHOOOOO-YIPPEEEYIPPPEEEEYAAAAAHOOOOOO! watch for Pan out of the corners of your eyes. You might see him, close by and up to his old tricks.